MW01644154

THE ULTIMATE FU

QUIZZES, QUESTI

JOURNAL PAGES & MORE!

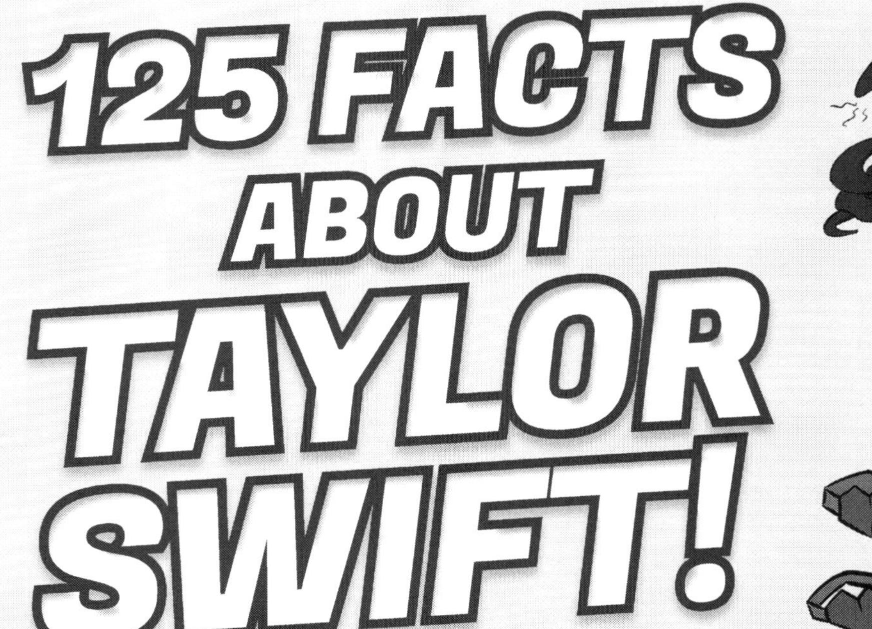

125 FACTS ABOUT TAYLOR SWIFT!

JESSICA BROWN

Copyright © 2024 by Screen Free Fun LLC

All rights reserved. No part of this publication may be reproduced, distributed, or transmitted in any form or by any means, including photocopying, recording, or other electronic or mechanical methods, without the prior written permission of the publisher, except in the case of brief quotations embodied in critical reviews and certain other noncommercial uses permitted by copyright law.

Screen Free Fun LLC
2111 S. Magnolia Ave
Tucson, AZ 85711

This book is unofficial and unauthorized. It is not authorized, approved, licensed, or endorsed by Taylor Swift, her management, or any record label or affiliate publishing companies. This book has been written in appreciation of Taylor Swift and her music and is intended for entertainment purposes only.

First Edition, 2024

Library of Congress Cataloging-in-Publication Data is available upon request.

Printed in the United States of America

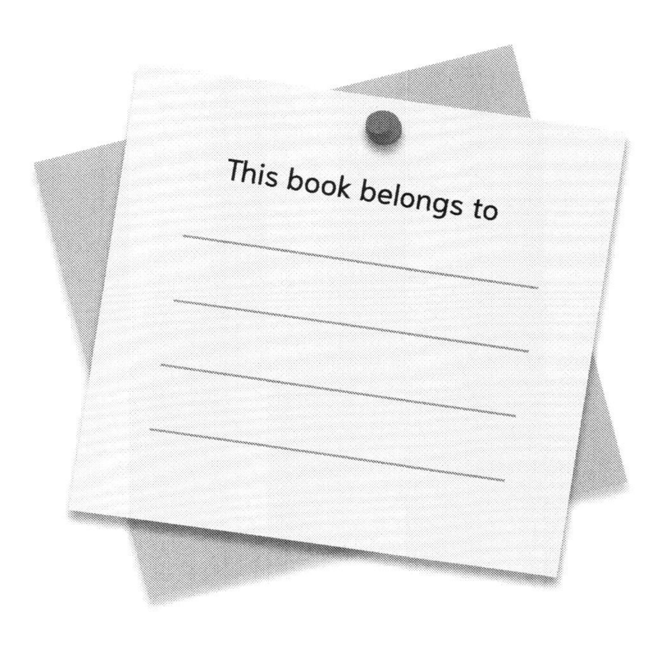
This book belongs to

FOREWORD

If you picked this book up, chances are you're either a hardcore Swiftie or you're about to become one. Taylor Swift isn't just a singer; she's a phenomenon—she's the music industry!

From her country roots to topping the pop charts, and then some, she's done it all. And let's be honest, she's pretty awesome at telling stories that hit you right in the feels.

This book will serve as your backstage pass to Taylor's world. Ever wondered about the stories behind those catchy tunes? Or how about the milestones that turned Taylor from a regular kid with big dreams into one of the biggest names in music? Well, you're in the right place.

With pages full of facts you might know and stuff you didn't know you needed to know, "125 Facts About Taylor Swift!: The Ultimate Fun Swiftie Fan Book- Quizzes, Questions, Quotes, Trivia, Journal Pages & More!" is all about fun—you may even find a few surprises along the way!

You'll be met with quizzes to test how well you really know Taylor, journal pages to spill your thoughts, and trivias that'll make you the go-to Swift expert. There's every bit of something for any kind of fan here.

Think of this book as hanging out with other Swifties, sharing your favorite Taylor moments, and celebrating everything that makes her music so special. From her debut album to "Midnights," it's a journey through the ups, downs, and everything in between.

So, grab a snack, wear those friendship bracelets, put on your favorite track, and get ready for a ride through the life and times of Taylor Swift. This book is a high-five to her and to every fan who's ever sung along at the top of their lungs to her songs.

Welcome to the ultimate Swiftie fan experience. Let the adventure begin!

TABLE OF CONTENTS

Part I. Taylor's Early Years

Biography of Taylor Swift's Early Life 6
Fact Attack: The Significance of the Number 13 7
Journal Page: My Favorite Number And Why 8
Quiz: How Well Do You Know Young Taylor? 10
Taylor's First Steps in Music 11
Taylor's Poem "A Monster in my Closet!" 13
Journal Page: Make Your Own Poem 14
Fact Attack: Taylor's Early Career Milestones 16

Part II. Albums Deep Dive

"Taylor Swift" Albums Timeline 18
Debut 20
Fearless 22
Speak Now 24
Red 26
1989 28
Reputation 30
Lover 33
folklore 35
evermore 37
Midnights 39
Quiz: Guess the Album! 41
Journal Page: "My Favorite Taylor Swift Album and Why" 43

Part III. Tours and Performances

Taylor's Tours Throughout the Years 44
Iconic Performances 45
Quiz: Taylor Swift Tour Trivia 47
Behind-the-Scenes Tour Facts 49
Taylor's Stage Styles 51
Taylor's Best Song Covers Performed 53
Build A Taylor Swift Concert 55
Draw Your Outfit! 56

Part IV. Collaborations and Influences

Famous Collaborations 57
Taylor's Musical Influences 59
Quiz: Guess the Collaborator 60

Part V. Fun Facts and Hidden Messages

Taylor's Love for Secret Messages 63
Spot the Easter Egg 65
The Art of Taylor's Lyrics 66
The Fictional Stories Behind Taylor's Songs 68
Which Taylor Swift Song Character Are You? 70
Journal Page: "Lyrics That Speak to Me" 72
More Fact Attacks About Taylor Swift 74
Taylor's Most Inspirational Quotes 76

Part VI. Quizzes, Questions, and More

Crossword 80
Taylor Recipe #1: Chai Sugar Cookies With Eggnog Icing 82
Taylor Recipe #2: Spaghetti and Meatballs 84
Word Search Puzzles 86
Creating Your Taylor Swift Playlist 88
Journal Page: "What I Would Say to Taylor" 90
Answer Key 92

TAYLOR'S EARLY DAYS

The Power Of Not Giving Up!

Taylor Swift's rise to fame started in the small town of Reading, Pennsylvania, where she was born on December 13, 1989. Taylor started to love music the moment she could put words together, making up her own songs by age five. She had a talent for turning feelings into songs, and she really wanted to share this with everyone!

Knowing how big Nashville is in the country music world, Taylor and her family decided to make a big move. They went to Nashville, Tennessee, when Taylor was only fourteen. This move was driven by her dream to be a singer-songwriter, and Nashville was the place she thought her dreams could really start.

However, Taylor's path wasn't so smooth there. She spent her days visiting music studios, guitar in hand, eager to play her music for anyone willing to hear it. It was a real test of sticking to it and loving what she does, and Taylor didn't give up. She understood that getting turned down was just part of the journey to making it.

Eventually, Taylor's steady effort finally paid off! She didn't just become a singer; she became a symbol of sticking to your dreams and being brave, no matter what. Her early life story shows us all a powerful message: with hard work, believing in yourself, and the bravery to face tough times, you can reach your dreams.

Taylor Swift, who started as a young girl with big dreams in a small town, turned into a worldwide music star, encouraging young girls everywhere to go after their dreams with the same passion.

How about you, what is your dream?

____

____

____

Fact Attack

What's With The Number 13?

13 Ways Taylor Is Connected To Her Favorite Number!

"I was born on the 13th, I turned 13 on Friday the 13th, my first album went gold in 13 weeks. Also, my first song that ever went number 1, it had a 13 second intro, I didn't even do that on purpose!

1. During her initial two tours, Taylor Swift used to mark her hand with the number 13 using eyeliner before performing.
2. "**Teardrops on My Guitar**", "**White Horse**", "**Ours**", "**Gorgeous**", and "**Mastermind**" by Taylor Swift each reached the 13th position on the Billboard Hot 100.
3. In the "**ME!**" music video, one scene features thirteen clouds.
4. Taylor Swift's debut chart-topping track on the Billboard Country Chart, "**Our Song**", begins with an intro lasting thirteen seconds.
5. "**The Lucky One**", track number thirteen on her "**Red**" album, starts with a thirteen-second introduction, and the song mentions "**lucky**" thirteen times.
6. Her Twitter handle is @taylorswift13, which comprises thirteen characters.
7. In the "**Ours**" music video, Taylor Swift's office cubicle is located on the 13th floor.
8. A poster of Taylor Swift's 1989 album makes an appearance in an episode of the Netflix series "**13 Reasons Why**", a show produced by her friend Selena Gomez.
9. Taylor Swift secured thirteen awards in 2018.
10. "**Fearless (Taylor's Version)**" was unveiled on February 11, 2021 (2+11=13), and it came out on April 9, 2021 (4+9=13).
11. The extended version of "**All Too Well**" runs for ten minutes and thirteen seconds.
12. The "**Bejeweled**" music video features an elevator with thirteen buttons.
13. Taylor Swift's albums "**Fearless**", "**1989**", and "**Midnights**", each containing thirteen tracks in their standard editions, have all received the Album of the Year award.

8

The Magic Of Lucky Numbers

Just as Taylor Swift's fondness for the number 13 has brought her luck and success over the years, do you have a number that seems to consistently bring you good fortune? Let's talk about it!

What is your favorite number? Write it down in BIG, BOLD digits!

Can you remember when this number first became significant to you? Was it something random, or does it have a deeper meaning? Share the story or moment that made this number stand out to you.

The Magic Of Lucky Numbers

Draw or design something creative around your favorite number. It could be a pattern, a doodle that incorporates the number, or even a short poem or song lyrics about it.

If you could associate your favorite number with a goal or dream for the future, what would it be? For example, if your favorite number is 7, maybe you dream of visiting the 7 wonders of the world!

What do you think about Taylor Swift's connection to the number 13? Do you find it interesting, inspiring, or just a fun coincidence?

QUIZ TIME!

How Well Do You Know Young Taylor?

Where was Taylor Swift born?
A) Nashville, Tennessee
B) Reading, Pennsylvania
C) Los Angeles, California
D) New York, New York

At what age did Taylor start making up her own songs?
A) Three
B) Five
C) Seven
D) Ten

Why did Taylor and her family move to Nashville, Tennessee?
A) For her father's job
B) To be closer to family
C) Because of Taylor's dream to be a singer-songwriter
D) For a change of scenery

What was one of the biggest challenges Taylor faced when she first moved to Nashville?
A) Finding a school
B) Making new friends
C) Getting music studios to listen to her music
D) Learning to play the guitar

What powerful message does Taylor Swift's early life story convey?
A) Fame comes easily to those with talent
B) Hard work, belief in oneself, and bravery are key to achieving dreams
C) Moving to a new city guarantees success
D) Music is a hobby, not a career

Taylor Swift's

First Steps in Music

A Star in the Making

Long before Taylor Swift became a household name with her catchy tunes and heartfelt lyrics, she was just a girl with a big dream—and an even bigger ambition. By the age of 10, she was already performing at local events and karaoke contests, showcasing her natural talent and passion for storytelling through music.

The Spark of Inspiration

Taylor's inspiration to pursue music professionally came from an unlikely source—a computer repairman. When she was just 12 years old, a technician who came to fix the family's computer taught her three chords on the guitar. Those three chords were all she needed to start crafting her own songs, turning her youthful experiences and vivid imagination into music that resonated with her (and millions of people!), even at such a tender age.

Taylor Swift's First Steps in Music

A Star Is Born

Taylor's hard work paid off when she caught the attention of Scott Borchetta, who was in the process of forming Big Machine Records. Impressed by her talent and determination, Borchetta signed Taylor, making her one of the first artists on his new label. In 2006, at just 16 years old, Taylor Swift released her self-titled debut album. The lead single, **"Tim McGraw,"** was a heartfelt ode to summer love and goodbyes, setting the stage for Taylor's meteoric rise to fame.

Swift's Signature Sound

From the beginning, Taylor's music stood out for its autobiographical nature. She penned songs that felt deeply personal, yet universally relatable, joining her country roots with pop tunes—a formula that would become her signature. Her talent in storytelling , combined with her ability to connect with fans on a personal level, quickly turned her into a beloved figure in the music industry!

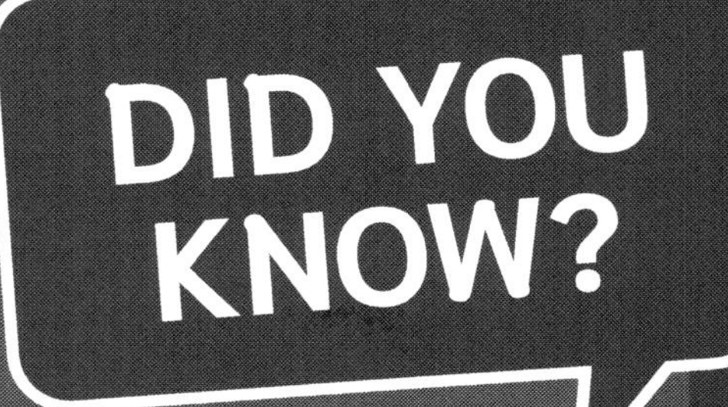

Taylor won a national poetry contest when she was just in fourth grade! Here's the exact poem that bagged her award:

A Monster In My Closet!

There's a monster in my closet and I don't know what to do!
Have you ever seen him?
Has he ever pounced on you?
I wonder what he looks like!
Is he purple with red eyes?
I wonder what he likes to eat.
What about his size!!
Tonight I'm gonna catch him!
I'll set a real big trap!
Then I'll train him really well.
He'll answer when I clap!

When I looked up in that closet, there was nothing there but stuff.
I know that monster's in there!
I heard him huff and puff!
Could it be he wants to eat me?
Maybe I'm his favorite tray.
And if he comes to get me,
I'll scream loudly, "Go away!!"
If he's nice, I'll name him "Happy."
If he's bad I'll name him "Grouch."
I suspect that he is leaving, but if not. . .I'll kick him out!

Unleash Your Inner Songwriter with Your Very Own Poem!

Taylor's poem *"A Monster In My Closet!"* was just the start of her incredible journey into music and storytelling. Now, it's your turn to tap into your inner Taylor Swift and create a poem of your own.

Who knows? This could be the first step on your path to becoming a songwriter!

Let's Brainstorm...

Think about something that excites you, scares you, makes you happy, or even something that makes you a little bit sad. It could be anything from your pet, a dream you had, an adventure with your friends, or like Taylor, even something in your closet!

Now, where does your poem take place? In a magical kingdom far away, under your bed, in a spooky forest, or perhaps in your own backyard? Paint a picture with your words so your readers can see the world you're creating.

What do you feel when you think about your poem? Are you excited, scared, joyful, or curious? Use those feelings to add emotion to your poem, making it come alive.

If you're ready, put pen to paper and let your words flow. Don't worry about making it perfect. Just let your ideas and emotions pour out.

Remember, Taylor Swift started with a simple poem, and look where she is now!

Your Creative Space

This page is your canvas. Write your poem here, draw pictures to go with it, or jot down any ideas that come to mind. There's no right or wrong way to be creative. So dream big, write from the heart, and start your journey to becoming a songwriter today!

Fact Attack

Taylor's Early Career Milestones

Debut Album Success

Taylor Swift's self-titled debut album was released on October 24, 2006. It stayed on the Billboard 200 chart for 277 weeks, making Taylor one of the youngest solo artists to write and record a #1 hit on the Hot Country Songs chart.

"Tim McGraw" Touchdown

The debut single "Tim McGraw," released in 2006, was inspired by a high school romance. It peaked at No. 6 on the Billboard Country charts, serving as a significant first step into the limelight.

A Teenage Record Breaker

At 17, Taylor became the youngest artist ever to win the Nashville Songwriters Association's Songwriter/Artist of the Year award in 2007, a record that she broke again in 2010.

Opening for Legends

Before her headlining tours, Taylor opened for country music legends like George Strait, Kenny Chesney, Tim McGraw, and Faith Hill during the early years of her career, showcasing her talent to a broad audience.

Platinum Plaudits

Taylor's debut album went multi-platinum, eventually selling over 5 million copies in the U.S. alone. This success was a testament to her widespread appeal and songwriting talent.

Fact Attack

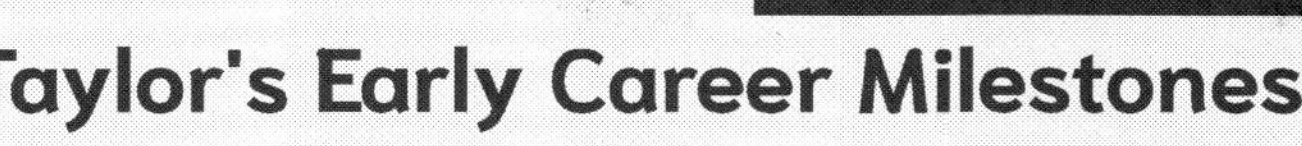

Taylor's Early Career Milestones

First Grammy Nods

Taylor earned her first Grammy Award nominations in 2008, including a Best New Artist nod. This recognition from the music industry's highest award was a clear sign of her budding career.

Youngest Album of the Year Winner

At the 52nd Grammy Awards, Taylor, at 20 years old, became the youngest ever winner of the Album of the Year award for "Fearless"—a record she held until 2020 (Billie Eilish beat it!).

Billboard's Youngest Top Country Artist

In 2009, Taylor was named Billboard's youngest-ever Female Artist of the Year, showcasing her ability to resonate with fans across generations.

MTV Video Music Award Controversy

Taylor's debut album went multi-platinum, eventually selling over 5 million copies in the U.S. alone. This success was a testament to her widespread appeal and songwriting talent.

"You Belong With Me"

The single "You Belong With Me" became Taylor's first top-5 hit on the Billboard Hot 100, solidifying her status as a crossover artist and showcasing her storytelling talent that appealed to a broad audience.

Now that you're well-prepped with knowledge and facts about Taylor's early life—let's dive into the masterpieces that allow us to have a glimpse of her stories of love, heartbreak, self-discovery, and resilience.

Reputation (2017)
With "Reputation," Swift took a darker, more edgy turn,

1989 (2014)
Fully embracing pop, "1989" was a sonic love letter to the '80s, brimming with synths and catchy hooks.

Folklore (2020) & Evermore (2020)
2020 was a year of surprise and introspection

Fearless (2008)
Two years later, Taylor released "Fearless," an album that catapulted her into the stratosphere of music royalty.

Taylor Swift (2006)
Kicking off our journey in 2006, Taylor Swift's debut album, "Taylor Swift," introduced the world to a fresh-faced country singer with dreams as big as her hair.

Taylor Swift's Albums Timeline

Here's a rundown of Taylor's first ten albums that made her one of the most celebrated artists in the industry!

Midnights (2022)
"Midnights," is a reflective dive into the sleepless nights of Taylor's life. With this album, she continues to explore new sounds while delivering the sharp, introspective lyrics she's known for.

reflecting on themes of love, media portrayal, and personal battles.

as Taylor released not one, but two indie-folk-inspired albums, "Folklore" and "Evermore."

Lover (2019)
"Lover" felt like a breath of fresh air, a return to the romantic, whimsical Taylor, with a mature twist.

Red (2012)
"Red" marked a bold departure from Taylor's country roots, blending pop, rock, and electronic elements.

Speak Now (2010)
"Speak Now," entirely written by Taylor herself, is a testament to her growing artistry and independence.

The Start of it All

A lot of emotions and heartbreak happen in high school—a canon event for the fragile hearts that grew up to be hopeless romantics. That's exactly what Taylor's debut album is about—it was like a teenager's journal, full of stories about the ups and downs of young love and life, filled with hope and deep feelings. With hits like "Teardrops on My Guitar," who are we to ignore such a classic masterpiece?

Classics from the Debut Album

"Tim McGraw" 3:52 •••

Would you believe that Taylor thought about writing this track during math class? Well, this song was actually about a guy she was dating but she knew they had to break it off once he went to college!

"Teardrops on My Guitar" 3:23 •••

Ever had a crush on a guy—and you actually never confessed? This song's the one for you—just replace your crush's name in the place of Drew!

"Our Song" 3:20 •••

With its upbeat tempo and catchy lyrics, "Our Song" became an instant hit. Who wouldn't love it—with a catchy melody that tells a very visual story, anyone who comes across this tune surely gets mesmerized.

"Picture to Burn" 2:53 •••

This fiery, upbeat track about moving on from a past relationship with a bit of sass and spite became our favorite breakup anthem. It was the perfect song to express teenage breakup angst!

"Should've Said No" 4:01 •••

Taylor wrote this song's chorus in just five minutes—with the anger of a young girl that discovered her boyfriend betrayed her. Fun fact: she actually based the lyrics on some of the words that she did use when she confronted her ex-boyfriend!

Fact Attack

Taylor Swift's Debut Domination

Taylor wrote or co-wrote every song on her debut album, mostly during her freshman year of high school, turning her diary into a chart-topping record.

Taylor didn't need to experience love firsthand to write about it; she crafted songs based on her observations, proving you don't need to date someone to write a heart-wrenching ballad about them.

All five singles from the album—"Tim McGraw," "Teardrops on My Guitar," "Our Song," "Picture to Burn," and "Should've Said No"—were certified platinum by the RIAA.

Beyond its success in the United States, "Taylor Swift" also charted in Australia, Canada, and the United Kingdom, hinting at Taylor's future as an international superstar.

True to her later albums, Taylor began her tradition of hiding messages in the lyrics' capital letters, offering fans an intimate glimpse into the stories behind the songs, a practice that would become a beloved part of her album releases. (We'll get to this later!)

Taylor wrote "Our Song" for a school talent show without any intention of it becoming a professional recording.

22

Facing Life With

All things glittery and gold come in the form of “Fearless,” a classic masterpiece of Taylor’s that featured her country roots, stories of romance, confessions, and the bittersweet taste of growing up. Taylor in this era was truly fearless—just imagine putting your ex-boyfriend on blast in national TV for breaking up with you over the phone! (Sorry Joe Jonas, we’re with Taylor on this one.)

Favorites From ‘Fearless’

♫ **"Love Story"** 3:55 •••

A modern-day Romeo and Juliet story, this track catapulted Taylor into the mainstream spotlight—everyone loves a good ol’ storytelling paired with a country tune!

♫ **"You Belong With Me"** 3:51 •••

This anthem became the soundtrack of many who was yearning for someone who already had a partner—who are we to compete when they wear short skirts and we just wear t-shirts, right?

♫ **"The Way I Loved You”** 4:03 •••

One of Taylor’s most addicting choruses, this song just makes us drown in all of our feels! This is yet another example of how Taylor could pull such a specific moment and turn it into a gut-wrenching song that we love to scream at the top of our lungs.

♫ **“The Other Side Of The Door”** 3:58 •••

Ever had those situations when what you’re acting on the outside is actually different from what you feel inside? This song definitely takes the cake for letting us be our dramatic selves—plus that outro is just so addicting to sing!

♫ **“Mr. Perfectly Fine”** 4:37 •••

Fans believe this is a direct hit to Taylor’s then-boyfriend Joe Jonas and was released as a vault track in 2021. Let’s just say, we can’t believe she kept this masterpiece from us all those years!

Fact Attack

Fearless on TOP!

"**Love Story**," one of Taylor's most iconic tracks, offers a creative twist on Shakespeare's tragic tale, "**Romeo and Juliet**," by giving it a happier ending.

The song "**Hey Stephen**" is a result of a mutual musical admiration between Taylor and Love And Theft's Stephen Barker Liles, with both artists penning songs about each other simultaneously.

"**Fearless**" not only captivated hearts worldwide but also secured its place as the fourth best-charting album of all time on Billboard's list.

When Taylor discovered that her heartfelt song "**White Horse**" would be featured on "**Grey's Anatomy**," she was moved to tears by the news.

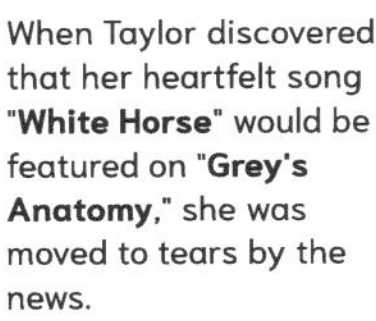

At the time, Taylor Swift set a record as the youngest solo artist to ever win a GRAMMY for Album of the Year with "**Fearless.**"

Taylor independently wrote seven out of the thirteen tracks on "**Fearless**," showcasing her solo creative talent.

The platinum edition of "**Fearless**" is notable for including Taylor's first studio recording of a song by another artist. Her version of Luna Halo's "**Untouchable**" was distinctively reimagined with altered verses and a more country-flavored arrangement.

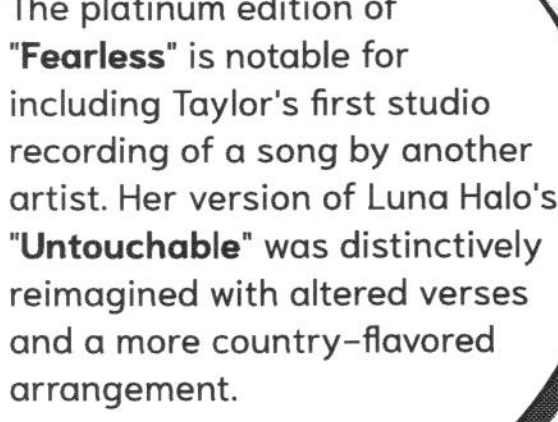

Dare To Speak With

If there's one album that could prove Taylor's unmatched songwriting skills, it would definitely be this one—she wrote the entirety of "Speak Now" all by herself! The songs in this weren't just simply about heartbreak; Taylor managed to uproot all the emotions and feelings we never imagined to put into words with such ease that this further cemented her reputation as a songwriter to watch out for! And spoiler alert: it's a no-skip album.

Storytelling Masterpieces From 'Speak Now'

♫ **"Mine"** 3:51 •••
This song comes off as a promising first track; it paints a picture of a relationship with the typical ups and downs, but Taylor does it so well and so romantically that it's easy to get hooked right at the first listen.

♫ **"Sparks Fly"** 4:21 •••
Sparks, butterflies, and kissing in the rain—this is what the song is essentially all about. It's the ultimate love song for those who love falling in love!

♫ **"Back to December"** 4:54 •••
This heartfelt apology song shows a more vulnerable side of Taylor, reflecting on a past relationship with regret. Sincerity and maturity are evident in the lyrics, resonating with the pain of realizing one's mistakes in love.

♫ **"Long Live"** 5:17 •••
You could always count on Taylor when it comes to making her fans feel loved—and this song's the perfect proof of it. This definitely goes down as one of her most classic songs, one that we're all sure to blast on our speakers even 50 years later.

♫ **"Mean"** 3:58 •••
If you need to prove someone wrong and pettily so, then "Mean" would just be the right song for you! This was written for Taylor's mean naysayers and, well, look at where she's at now.

♫ **"The Story of Us"** 4:27 •••
The ultimate "yikes" feeling summed up into a song—no one really knows what to do with the awkwardness of running into an ex.

Fact Attack

The Sensation That Is “Speak Now”!

“**Dear John,**” which ran for almost 7 minutes, used to be Taylor’s longest song—until it was broken by **“All Too Well (10 Minute Version)”** in 2021.

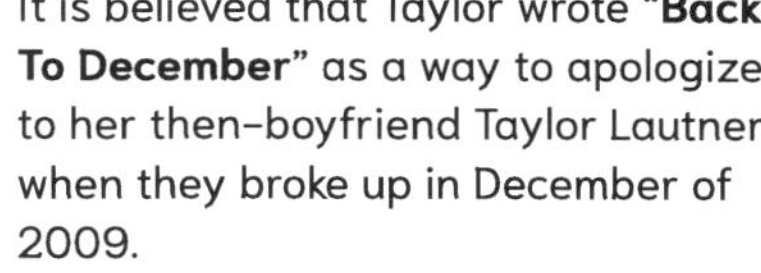

It is believed that Taylor wrote “**Back To December**” as a way to apologize to her then-boyfriend Taylor Lautner when they broke up in December of 2009.

The album was supposed to be called “**Enchanted**” instead of “**Speak Now**” because Scott Borcheta wanted a more mature title.

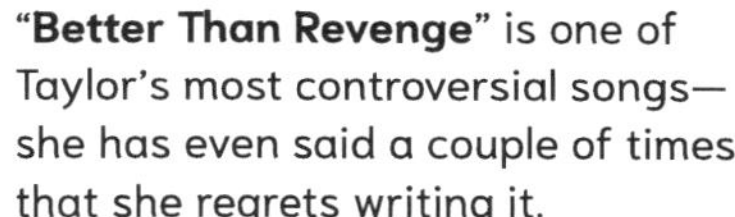

“**Better Than Revenge**” is one of Taylor’s most controversial songs—she has even said a couple of times that she regrets writing it.

Taylor already sang “**Sparks Fly**” on her shows three years before “**Speak Now**” was released—fans wanted to hear it again, so she put it on the album.

“**Speak Now**” bagged 2 trophies at the Grammies, and it was also nominated for Best Country Solo Performance and Song for “**Mean**.”

“**The Story of Us**” cleverly uses the phrases “*Next chapter*“ and “*The end*” to highlight the story aspect of the song’s lyrics.

Taylor wrote “**Never Grow Up**” when she moved out of her parents’ house to a million-dollar condo in Nashville, Tennessee.

RAGING RED

Like the color itself, “Red” comes with a lot of emotional turmoil and deep feelings that are anchored to very specific happenings in Taylor’s life—which a lot of us beautifully relate to, too! With prominent themes of heartbreak, fleeting romances, and a lot of looking back, it successfully shows the shades of experiences that the title suggests—passion, anger, and everything in between.

Fan-Favorite Songs Of Heartbreak and Musings from “Red”

"All Too Well" 5:29 •••

Perhaps the crown jewel of "Red," "All Too Well" has earned legendary status among fans and critics alike—everyone liked it so much they kept asking for the 10-minute original version of it! Good thing Taylor loves her fans so much and eventually gave us the longer version of this song when she released “Red (Taylor’s Version)”.

"I Knew You Were Trouble" 3:39 •••

Anyone who’s had a rocky relationship with someone knows the sentiments that this song brings—it perfectly describes the feeling of falling for someone who is bad news!

"We Are Never Ever Getting Back Together" 3:13 •••

The title may be long, but it became an instant hit and rightfully so. The song’s playful melody and fun chorus cemented it as a sing-along favorite at parties!

"22" 3:51 •••

Nothing makes 21-year-olds excited than wait for their 22nd birthdays because they get to use this song to celebrate it! It’s definitely a go-to for parties—or even just when you want to reflect on your youth.

"Message in a Bottle" 3:46 •••

Taylor proves once again that she’s the master of coming up with the perfect lyrics for a seemingly unattainable crush—this song’s the perfect jam for all those yearning for someone who may not reciprocate their feelings back.

"Red" 3:43 •••

The title track, "Red," incredibly uses figures of speech in the lyrics, comparing love to different shades of colors—all in a beautiful mix of country and pop tunes that has turned into an earworm for many of us. It’s the perfect title track representing everything in the album!

Fact Attack

The Ever-Iconic "Red"

Taylor was surprised by the massive following "**All Too Well**" garnered.

Taylor initially penned around **40 songs** for "Red."

"**Red**" is considered Taylor Swift's definitive break-up album.

The album "**Red**" was partly inspired by Joni Mitchell's "Blue."

"**We Are Never Ever Getting Back Together**" from "**Red**" earned Swift her first #1 on the Billboard Hot 100.

Fans speculate "**All Too Well**" references actor Jake Gyllenhaal.

Taylor Swift found the re-release of "**Red**" more enjoyable, contrasting with her emotional struggles during its initial launch.

With "**I Knew You Were Trouble**," Taylor Swift embraced a dubstep vibe, showcasing a departure from her country roots.

"Sad Beautiful Tragic" was written by Taylor on a bus, reflecting on the wistful loss of a past relationship.

Party Like It's 1989 !!

An album that takes you to the city (Welcome to New York—duh!) and beach adventures, "1989" is Taylor's first official entry to pop world. It stands as an iconic departure from her country roots, with hits that lean on more to synth- and electro-pop sounds. Taylor didn't only reinvent her musical identity in this era, but she also set a new standard for pop excellence—this's album's called the 'pop bible' for a reason!

Pop Wonders In "1989"

"Blank Space" 3:51 •••

Taylor has always been branded as a serial dater—so she did the most Taylor thing: she wrote a song about it, flipped the narrative, and ironically owned that persona the media made her out to be! With an irresistibly catchy melody and lines that are full of satire and sass, it's the perfect snapback to the industry that thinks she's just a good-for-nothing heartbreaker.

"Style" 3:50 •••

Nothing screams more pop than Taylor's song "Style"—the beat? Catchy! The lyrics? Swoon-worthy! Not to mention it's also allegedly about *wink* Harry Styles.

"Shake It Off" 3:38 •••

Leave it to Taylor to deal with critics who hate her awkward dancing with a music video of her awkwardly dancing! But on a deeper level, this song makes us value self-acceptance in the midst of worries and criticisms—when in doubt, just dance away and shake it off!

"How You Get The Girl" 4:06 •••

This one's for the boys who seem to have no idea on how to make the first move—this song's chorus already tells you everything that you need to do. Really, that's just how it works, that's how you get the girl!

"You Are In Love" 4:26 •••

Taylor wrote this song for one of her closest friends (and producer!) Jack Antonoff, when he was in a relationship with American writer Lena Dunham. She described the track Jack sent her as "the sound of like, actual love—true love" and immediately wrote the lyrics for it—leaving us with one of her most romantic love songs ever released.

Fact Attack

Taylor's Golden "1989" Era

"**This Love**" was penned prior to the launch of "**Red**."

The heartbeat in "**Wildest Dreams**" is actually Taylor's.

Taylor was inspired to write "**All You Had to Do Was Stay**" after a dream where she could only emit a high-pitched, operatic "**Stay**!" instead of speaking when her ex showed up.

Before its release, Taylor shared the original "**1989**" album with a select group of friends, including Karlie Kloss, Lena Dunham, Ed Sheeran, and Lorde.

Diane Warren, who collaborated on "**Say Don't Go**," confirmed that the song's lyrics remained unchanged from their original version in 2014.

Taylor has described "**Is It Over Now?**" as sister songs of "Out of the Woods" and "**I Wish You Would**."

Taylor joined Whitney Houston as the only female artists to have multiple albums remain at the top of the Billboard 200 chart for at least 10 weeks because of "**1989**."

The distinctive snare sound in "**Out of the Woods**" is a combination of white noise from a blown EMI board, hand claps, and the sound of Jack Antonoff dropping his gear bag, all meticulously recorded.

"**1989**" boasted sales of 1,287,000 in its first week, outperforming the combined sales of the next 100 titles on the Billboard 200 for the week ending November 2.

The Daring REPUTATION

Don't let "Reputation's" aesthetic fool you—behind it's brooding and more daring musical tone, it's actually considered as one of Taylor's most romantic and intimate albums. She leaves us with a more vulnerable glimpse into her feelings, proving that love can flourish even amidst her being a subject of public scrutiny. The album's color may be black, but the songs are full of colorful imagery that we can't always get enough of when we hit the play button!

Romance in Reputation: Songs On Replay

"Look What You Made Me Do" 3:31 •••
Nothing beats this from being the perfect comeback song after being the subject of heavily-biased public criticism—Taylor shut all the haters up with this edgy tune. Look what you made her do!

"Delicate" 3:52 •••
Vulnerable love—this is what the song's all about. In the midst of the whole world seemingly turning its back on Taylor, she leaves a quite meek tune to her lover with lyrics that say, "You must like me for me." Who wouldn't want that kind of love?

"Gorgeous" 3:29 •••
This song is definitely the perfect one to play when you're swooning over someone and you're mind is too clouded with thoughts to even approach or talk to them. Taylor says it in the song herself, "You're so gorgeous, I can't say anything to your face!"

"Getaway Car" 3:53 •••
Who doesn't love a little adventure? This song takes us on—well, a getaway car of emotions that keeps us hanging. If you want a little bit of escape without leaving your seat, this song's a safe go-to.

"King of my Heart" 3:34 •••
Yet another song that testifies Taylor's knack for making the feeling of falling head over heels in love like the best thing in the world. This song takes us on a whirlwind of feels—we just love it when our 'American Queen' is brimming with love!

Want More Facts That You Won't Find Anywhere Else?

Unlock 31 Taylor Swift facts that you can't find online!

Plus, you'll get a free 55-page bonus Taylor Swift activity book full of tons of extra activities.

Scan the QR code or use the link below to get your bonuses now!

www.swiftiesuperfans.com/freebies

Fact Attack
When "Reputation" Rocked Us All Out

Taylor Swift's "Reputation" zoomed to #1 on iTunes in just six minutes—she's called 'The Music Industry' for a reason!

Right after it came out, "Reputation" sold more than all the other top 199 albums combined, making new history.

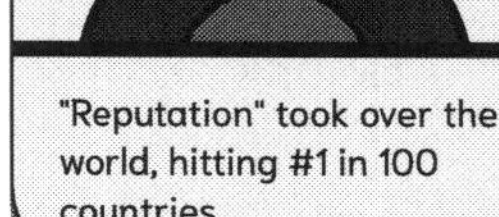

"Reputation" took over the world, hitting #1 in 100 countries.

The "Look What You Made Me Do" video broke records with 84.4 million first-week US views, the most for any female artist.

Taylor Swift was the first woman to perform twice at Ireland's Croke Park and the first to have three-night shows at both Gillette Stadium and MetLife Stadium in the US, also the first at Mile High Stadium.

The Reputation World Tour was sold out everywhere, bringing in a total of 2.9 million fans.

The huge setup for the Reputation Tour needed 80 trucks to move all the gear—well, you do get your money's worth when you buy tickets to a Taylor concert.

Taylor gave 2,000 adopted and foster kids free tickets to her final dress rehearsal —proving that her heart is just as big as her stadium tour!

Soft and Romantic

It's in the album name itself—"Lover" is all about being deeply in love with someone and addressing the fears and worries of losing something so special. Taylor takes us through the highs and lows of love, while also confronting the vulnerabilities that come with it. It's the perfect sequel transition from the romantic endings of her last album—she went from snakes into butterflies for this one!

Anthems of Love in "Lover"

"Lover" 3:41

If there's one this song is perfect for, it's definitely being the best wedding song choice for all the elder Swifties who have found their other halves already. "Lover" is also for the hopeless romantics—we can't ever listen to this song without swooning!

"Paper Rings" 3:42

Ever felt so in-love that you may as well just marry someone with paper rings? This song is for those moments when love feels so real and fun that even the simplest gesture means the world!

"Cornelia Street" 4:47

This track takes you on a nostalgic trip down memory lane, perfect for those who cherish memories of a love so strong it could survive anything. It's for anyone who's ever feared losing a place where they've experienced pure joy and love.

"Afterglow" 3:43

This one's ideal for those moments when you're reflecting on a fight or misunderstanding, realizing your own mistakes. When in doubt, just meet us in the afterglow!

"Daylight" 4:53

Often hailed as the complete opposite of "Red", this one's a beautiful ode to finding love that feels like daylight breaking after a long, dark night—symbolizing hope and a fresh start.

Fact Attack

"Lover" and Its Love-Struck Revelations!

Taylor decided "**Lover**" would be the album's title after writing the song, originally considering "**Daylight**."

The intro of "**London Boy**" features Idris Elba, taken from his chat on The Late Late Show with James Corden.

Taylor crafted every track on "**Lover**" uniquely for the album, ensuring no song was a holdover from past projects.

The concept for the "**Lover**" music video drew from "**You Are In Love**" lyrics, *"you two are dancing in a snow globe round and round."*

"**The Man**" tackles Swift's musings on how her career might differ if she were male.

Inspired by "**Someone Great**" on Netflix, "**Death By a Thousand Cuts**" was born.

"**It's Nice to Have A Friend**" includes the Regent Park School of Music youth choir, with sales proceeds supporting the school.

"**Soon You'll Get Better**" reflects on Andrea Swift's (Taylor's mom!) cancer fight, a track the family agreed to include on the album.

"**Cornelia Street**" stands out as one of Taylor Swift's personal favorites on "**Lover**."

The Fictional World of FOLKLORE

Taylor once again took the world by storm in 2020 when she released "folklore" in the midst of everyone in isolation—and showed us a completely different new style of music from her. "folklore" is like stepping into a secret world of stories and quiet reflections, as Taylor takes by hand into a place where tales of love, heartbreak, and finding oneself are wrapped in soft, haunting melodies; completely taking us away from her usual bubblegum pop tunes.

Ethereal Echoes of Folklore

"the 1" 3:30

A soft and mellow take on the concept of "the one that got away," this song wraps up wistful feelings and what-ifs in a melody that's both comforting and contemplative, perfect for those moments of reflection on past loves and the possibilities that never came to be.

"cardigan" 3:59

This one's for anyone who has ever felt the enduring connection of a first love, and the security of being remembered and cherished, much like an old cardigan, hence, the title!

"the last great american dynasty" 3:51

A storytelling masterpiece that recounts the whimsical and controversial life of Rebekah Harkness, the woman who once owned the house Taylor bought by the seaside!

"invisible string" 4:13

This song gently digs into the idea of luck and the hidden reasons people come into each other's lives. It's a tribute to the mysterious ways we connect with others, even when we can't explain why. Well, if it's meant to be, it will be!

"this is me trying" 3:15

An anthem of vulnerability and the effort it takes to overcome personal struggles, this song offers comfort to anyone who's ever felt like they're barely holding on but still pushing forward. It's a gentle reminder that trying, in itself, is a brave act of resilience.

"mirrorball" 3:29

This track shines with the longing to be seen and the adaptability of those who constantly change themselves to meet others' expectations. Eldest daughters, anyone?

Fact Attack

“Folklore” Fantasies

While everyone was trying new hobbies at home, Taylor Swift was busy creating her entire "**folklore**" album during lockdown. She started in April and put together all 16 songs, showing us a whole new side of her music.

Taylor took on a big challenge by directing the "**cardigan**" music video during quarantine. She followed all the health rules with masks and gloves to make sure everyone stayed safe while creating something beautiful.

The first song Taylor wrote for "**folklore**" was "**my tears ricochet**," and she did it all by herself. This song kicks off the emotional journey of the album.

Taylor didn't tell anyone she was working on "**folklore**," not even her friends!

Taylor included three special songs on "**folklore**" that tell the story of a love triangle from different points of view. Fans think these songs are "**betty**," "**cardigan**," and "**august**," each showing a different side of the story.

Taylor shared that "**cardigan**" is about looking back at a past love and understanding why it's so memorable. It's about those feelings that stick with us.

Taylor decided to hide clues and messages in the lyrics instead of just in her music videos. She built stories and connections throughout the album for fans to discover.

Taylor says "**folklore**" feels like a mix of new stories and the emotional depth of her song "**Sad, Beautiful, Tragic**" from the "**Red**" album.

37

"folklore's" elder sister, EVERMORE

As if surprising us mid-pandemic wasn't enough, Taylor went ahead and saved the year 2020 even more when she dropped yet another surprise album called "evermore." While "folklore" exuded spring and summer vibes, Taylor made a sister album that's all about fall and winter. With "evermore," Taylor not only continued to captivate her audience with her storytelling skills but also showed how versatile she is as an artist, proving she's truly one of the most creative and productive musicians in this generation!

Emotional Tales from "evermore"

"champagne problems" 4:04 •••
If you need proof that Taylor is truly a stellar songwriter that can whip up songs with such vivid imagery, then "champagne problems" is definitely the way to go.

"gold rush" 3:05 •••
A catchy tune about chasing after someone who seems to be wanted by everyone, "gold rush" captures the excitement of pursuing someone shiny and new to everyone's eye.

"long story short" 3:35 •••
With its upbeat tempo, "long story short" sums up life's twists and turns in a simple, catchy way. It's the perfect song for those who finally found peace after everything life's thrown in their way!

"happiness" 5:15 •••
Taylor brings us to a whole new dimension of showing how happiness can be found even in heartbreak and also be a journey towards self-discovery and inner contentment.

"cowboy like me" 4:35 •••
This track spins a tale of two free spirits finding each other amidst life's chaos, painting a picture of adventure and connection.

"right where you left me" 4:05 •••
With haunting melodies and gut-wrenching lyrics, Taylor explores the aftermath of a breakup, capturing the feeling of being stuck in a moment frozen in time, waiting for closure.

Fact Attack

The Enigmatic Charm of "evermore"

Taylor revealed in The Long Pond Studio Sessions that William Bowery, previously a mysterious collaborator on "Folklore," was actually her then-partner Joe Alwyn, who co-wrote "Betty" and "Exile" on "evermore."

The inclusion of Olive Garden in "no body, no crime" was a nod to Este Haim's fondness for the restaurant—yes, the same Este that the song refers to!

The track "no body, no crime" featuring Haim was inspired by Swift's fascination with true crime podcasts and documentaries, showcasing her ability to blend personal interests with her music.

Both "folklore" and "evermore" feature a song dedicated to Taylor's grandparents on their respective 13th tracks —"epiphany" and "marjorie."

The music video for "willow" is linked to the "cardigan" video through a shared setting of a wooden cabin and a piano connected by a golden thread, reflecting the song's lyrical connection to "folklore's" "invisible string."

"Happiness" contains references to F. Scott Fitzgerald's "The Great Gatsby," demonstrating Taylor's knack for weaving literary allusions into her lyrics.

When Taylor released "evermore," it marked the first time she released two studio albums in the same calendar year and continued a musical era past one album with it being the "sister record" to "folklore."

Mayhem with MIDNIGHTS

Returning to her pop roots, Taylor concluded the era of sister albums with the synth-pop vibes of "Midnights" — proving yet once again that she can bounce back stronger than any '90s trend. She describes this album as a collection of her deepest thoughts during the sleepless nights of some of the different parts of her life—leading us to speculate who or what each song is about with fun!

"Midnights" Melodies We Can't Get Out Of Our Head

"Lavender Haze" 3:22 •••

Taylor explained that this song describes a love that is to be protected from the outside world—rooting her experiences from her then-six-year relationship with Joe Alwyn, which they have always been private about. To simply put it, she says that this song is "sort of about the act of ignoring that stuff to protect the real stuff."

"Maroon" 3:38 •••

Maroon is a deeper shade of "Red"—both the color and the song! Much like how the latter describes a love so deep and emotional, this song is also all about reflecting on the bittersweet memory of a relationship that has left a scarring mark so scarlet it was maroon (see what we did there?).

"Snow on the Beach" 4:16 •••

This one's all about falling in love with someone the same time they're also falling in love with you—described as the phenomenon of snow on the beach, basically saying that it's "weird, but it was beautiful." With the touch of Lana Del Rey's haunting voice, this song easily caught our hearts.

"You're On Your Own, Kid" 3:!4 •••

If you've ever wondered why so many fans trade friendship bracelets in Taylor's concerts, this song is to blame. With the lyric "So make the friendship bracelets..." this Track 5 single-handedly turned stadiums into bracelet trading spots for everyone!

"Bejeweled" 3:14 •••

Whenever you need an affirmation that you can shine on your own, here's a tune to blast and rock your head into—who wouldn't be motivated to march to their own beat while singing "Best believe I'm still bejeweled"?

Fact Attack
The Magic of "Midnights"

"**Midnights**" is a collection of songs inspired by things that kept Taylor up at night, like self-doubt, past loves, and dreams.

Actress Zoë Kravitz co-wrote the opening track "Lavender Haze."

The album achieved massive success, becoming Taylor's 11th consecutive number one album and landing all its songs in the Billboard Hot 100's top 10 for a week - a first for any artist!

"Midnights" was the best-selling album of 2022 and the second-best of 2023, making Taylor the first artist to achieve a yearly best-seller six times!

Speaking of "Lavender Haze," the drums are played by Dylan O'Brien (yes, the actor from "All Too Well: The Short Film!).

There's a "3am Edition" of the album with extra songs, all of which charted within the top 45 of the Billboard Hot 100.

The music videos and album aesthetic for "Midnights" hint at Taylor's past eras, with outfits referencing iconic looks from previous videos.

The "Midnights" rollout was full of Easter eggs, with cryptic lyrics revealed on billboards before the album release.

QUIZ TIME!

Guess The Taylor Swift Album

Which Taylor Swift album features the heartbreak anthem "**All Too Well**" and explores themes of passion, anger, and everything in between?

Known for the tracks "**Love Story**" and "**You Belong With Me**," this album set a record with Taylor Swift as the youngest solo artist to ever win a GRAMMY for Album of the Year. Which album is it?

This album is Taylor Swift's first official pop endeavor, featuring hits like "**Blank Space**" and "**Shake It Off**." Which album marked her iconic departure from country to pop?

Featuring the song "**champagne problems**" and continuing the storytelling saga started in its sister album, which Taylor Swift album is known for its fall and winter vibes?

With tracks like "**Look What You Made Me Do**" and "**Delicate**," this Taylor Swift album explores themes of love amidst public scrutiny. Which album is it?

QUIZ TIME!

Guess The Taylor Swift Album

- Featuring "Lover" and "Paper Rings," this album is all about the highs and lows of love. Which Taylor Swift album is it?

- Known for "Mine" and "Back to December," this album showcases Taylor Swift's unmatched songwriting skills as she wrote the entirety of it herself. Which album is this?

- With tracks like "Tim McGraw" and "Teardrops on My Guitar," this album is like a teenager's journal full of stories about young love. What is the name of Taylor Swift's debut album?

- This album features "Lavender Haze" and "Maroon," exploring deep thoughts during sleepless nights. What is the title of this Taylor Swift album?

- This Taylor Swift album is a reflective journey with songs like "the 1" and "cardigan," offering a new style of music. What is the album's title?

43

What is your favorite Taylor Swift album and why?

Taylor Swift's journey through music is a mosaic of emotions, stories, and melodies that speak to the heart of millions. From the country roots of her self-titled debut to the indie-folk tales of "folklore" and "evermore," each album unfolds a new chapter not just in Taylor's life but in ours too. Whether it's the heartfelt stories of "Speak Now," the pop anthems of "1989," or the romantic lyrics of "Lover," there's always a Taylor Swift album that feels like it was written just for you.

Write your favorite Taylor Swift album here!

- What makes this album stand out to you among Taylor's discography?
- Is there a particular memory or period in your life that this album soundtracks?
- How do the lyrics, melodies, or themes of the album resonate with your own experiences or dreams?
- Are there specific songs that you connect with on a deeper level? What are they and why?
- How has this album influenced your perspective on love, life, or yourself?

Taylor's Tours
Throughout The Years

2009–2010

Taylor Swift's Fearless Tour

Taylor's first headlining tour, promoting her second studio album, "Fearless." This tour was where Taylor began to make her mark as a live performer!

2011–2012

Speak Now World Tour

Supporting her third studio album, "Speak Now," this tour highlighted Taylor's ability to connect with fans through her songwriting. It was more theatrical, with elaborate sets and costumes that complemented her story-driven songs.

2013–2014

The Red Tour

Marking a significant shift towards pop, the Red Tour supported her fourth studio album, "Red." This tour was notable for its high energy, visually stunning stages, and the seamless blend of country roots with pop elements.

2015

The 1989 World Tour

Celebrating her first official pop album, "1989," this tour was a massive global success. It featured high-production value, numerous guest appearances, and set lists that included a mix of new hits and old favorites, fully embracing her pop transformation.

2018

Reputation Stadium Tour

In support of her sixth album, "Reputation," this tour was her most ambitious yet, with a massive stage setup, elaborate visuals, and a theme that addressed her media portrayal. It broke numerous records and showcased Taylor's resilience and ability to reinvent herself.

2023–

The Eras Tour

This huge tour is a celebration of her entire career, revisiting every album and era—testifying to her longevity and versatility as an artist. This tour not only highlights her musical journey but also reinforces her connection with fans across different phases of her career.

Did you know?

There was supposed to be a tour called **"Lover Fest"**—centering around her seventh album, **"Lover,"** but the world had other plans at that time (hint: the pandemic struck!).

Taylor's Best Performances

Scan these to view the performances!

"Should've Said No" at the AMA Awards
Back in 2008, when Taylor was just starting, she already made waves at the American Music Awards. Her performance of "Should've Said No," right from her first album, was a showstopper with an outfit change and rain on stage, hinting at the superstar she was destined to become.

"Out Of The Woods" at the Grammys
The 2016 Grammys opened with a bang as Taylor performed "Out Of The Woods." It was a powerful start to the night, and she even went home with three Grammys!

"Mean" at the Grammys
Taylor's "Mean" performance at the 2011 Grammys was a standout moment. After facing harsh criticism for a previous Grammy show, she came back with "Mean," earning a standing ovation and proving doubters wrong with her lyrics about rising above.

"Cornelia Street" Live From Paris
In Paris 2020, Taylor's acoustic rendition of "Cornelia Street" was magical. With just her guitar, she captivated everyone as the crowd lit up the night with their phones.

"I Did Something Bad" During Reputation Stadium Tour
During the Reputation Stadium Tour, Taylor's performance of "I Did Something Bad" was a highlight. Amidst controversy, she delivered a show full of stunning visuals and a fierce attitude, embodying the spirit of the album.

Taylor's Best Performances

Rock Version of "We Are Never Ever Getting Back Together"
On her 1989 Tour, Taylor rocked out with an electric guitar to a rock version of "We Are Never Ever Getting Back Together," showing her versatility beyond pop.

The Long Pond Studio Sessions
After releasing "folklore," Taylor's intimate performances in the accompanying documentary were a deep dive into the album's heartfelt lyrics, offering a glimpse into her vulnerability.

"All Too Well" on SNL
Taylor's long-awaited 10-minute version of "All Too Well" performed on SNL was an emotional masterpiece, showcasing her incredible storytelling ability.

folklore/evermore Medley at the Grammys
At the 2021 Grammys, Taylor performed a mesmerizing medley from "folklore" and "evermore," complete with a fairytale-like setting that captured the essence of both albums.

Artist of the Decade Performance at the 2019 AMAs
Taylor's medley at the 2019 AMAs celebrated her hits over the decade, proving why she was the Artist of the Decade. This performance hinted at the magic that "The Eras Tour" would bring.

QUIZ TIME!

Taylor's Tour Trivia

I

Which tour marked Taylor Swift's first time headlining?

- A Speak Now World Tour
- B Fearless Tour
- C The Red Tour
- D The 1989 World Tour

II

What was unique about the Speak Now World Tour?

- A It was entirely acoustic.
- B It featured elaborate sets and costumes.
- C It included only country songs.
- D It was performed in small venues only.

III

The Red Tour is known for blending which two music styles?

- A Pop and rock
- B Country and pop
- C Folk and country
- D Electronic and pop

IV

Which tour celebrated Taylor's first official pop album, "1989"?

- A The 1989 World Tour
- B The Reputation Stadium Tour
- C The Eras Tour
- D Lover Fest

V

The Reputation Stadium Tour mainly addressed which theme?

- A Love stories
- B The media's portrayal of Taylor
- C Childhood memories
- D Fairytales

VI

What was the planned tour for the "Lover" album that got canceled?

- A The Eras Tour
- B The 1989 World Tour
- C Lover Fest
- D Speak Now World Tour

VII

At which event did Taylor perform "Should've Said No" with rain on stage?

- A The Grammys
- B The AMAs
- C The VMAs
- D Billboard Music Awards

VIII

Which song did Taylor perform at the 2016 Grammys?

- A "Mean"
- B "Out Of The Woods"
- C "Cornelia Street"
- D "I Did Something Bad"

IX

Where did Taylor give an acoustic performance of "Cornelia Street"?

- A London
- B New York
- C Paris
- D Nashville

X

Which performance hinted at what "The Eras Tour" would be like?

- A "All Too Well" on SNL
- B Rock Version of "We Are Never Ever Getting Back Together"
- C Artist of the Decade Performance at the 2019 AMAs
- D folklore/evermore Medley at the Grammys

Fact Attack

Behind the Scenes of The Eras Tour

Taylor Swift started her Eras Tour with a huge show in Arizona, breaking the record for the most people at a concert by a female artist in the US with 69,000 fans.

In Seattle, Taylor's fans were so loud and excited they caused what was called a "2.3 magnitude earthquake" at the stadium during one of her concerts.

Taylor's guitar for the Fearless part of the concert was made special by her parents. They used super glue to add silver sparkles and a lucky number 13 to it.

Every night, Taylor gives away a special "22" hat made by the same person who made Lady Gaga's famous pink hat. She picks one fan to give it to.

For one of her Arizona shows, Taylor wore a special "Enchanted" dress that took over 350 hours to make

50

Fact Attack

Behind the Scenes of The Eras Tour

Another blue "Enchanted" dress she wore in LA took about 2,100 hours to make—this was when she announced the release of "1989 (Taylor's Version)."

The special outfit Taylor wears for the "Midnights" part of her show took 315 hours to make and is covered in over 5,300 sparkles.

The clothes Taylor wears for the Lover part of her show were made by Versace, a very famous fashion brand.

The person who designs the look of Taylor's show, Ethan Tobman, has worked with other big stars like Beyoncé and was the production designer of some movies like "Room," "The Menu," and more.

It takes about 90 big trucks to carry all the stuff needed for Taylor's show stage—imagine the struggle of carrying it across the globe for worldwide fans to experience "The Eras Tour!"

Taylor's *Stage Styles* Through The Eras

Taylor's fashion isn't just about looking good (which, let's be honest, she nails every time); it's a visual soundtrack to her musical evolution. From her roots in country to her reign in pop and indie, Taylor's outfits have been singing their own tunes, telling us where she's been and where she's headed!

- **Debut Era**

  Remember when Taylor was the girl next door with a guitar and dreams as big as her hair? Those cowboy boots and sundresses weren't just cute; they were the prologue to her story, setting the stage for everything that was to come.

- **Fearless Era**

  This is where the glitter started to stick. Taylor stepped up her game with dresses that sparkled like her eyes when she sings about first love.

- **Speak Now Era**

  Taylor, in her gowns and tiaras, wasn't just performing during the "Speak Now" era; she was inviting us into her enchanted world, filled with princes, castles, and a few dragons along the way.

- **Red Era**

  Taylor's Red era was like a chic coffee shop playlist—cool, sophisticated, and a little bit indie. Striped shirts, high-waisted shorts, and those iconic fedoras? A perfect blend of country roots and pop ambitions.

Taylor's *Stage Styles* Through The Eras

1989 Era

Metallics, crop tops, and sky-high heels were Taylor's uniform as she conquered the world, one synth-pop anthem at a time. This era was sleek, stylish, and all about embracing the spotlight.

Reputation Era

Things got real. Dark colors, leather, and an air of mystery defined the Reputation era. Taylor showed us her fierce side, with fashion that screamed confidence and a hint of rebellion.

Lover Era

After the storm comes the rainbow, right? The Lover era was a burst of pastel joy, sequins, and heart-shaped everything. Taylor reminded us that it's okay to wear your heart on your sleeve (or your dress).

Folklore/Evermore Era

Cue the cozy vibes. With Folklore and Evermore, Taylor went indie, and her style followed suit. Lace, cardigans, and earthy tones made her performances feel like intimate gatherings among friends.

Midnights Era

With sophisticated, glittery outfits, Taylor's exploring the complexities of fame, love, and self-discovery, one dazzling look at a time in this era.

Taylor's Best Song Covers

Aside from being a storytelling and songwriting machine, Taylor also has a knack of turning another artist's song into her own. Let's take a look at some of her best covers:

"How to Save a Life" by The Fray

Taylor gave an emotional performance in Denver, hitting low notes that surprised many!

"You Oughta Know" by Alanis Morissette

During her 1989 Tour, Taylor and Alanis rocked out together, proving Taylor's love for '90s hits.

"September" by Earth, Wind & Fire

Taylor went back to her country roots with a gentle cover on Spotify, even changing the date in the lyrics to make it her own.

"Ain't Nothin' Bout You" by Brooks & Dunn

Taylor honored the country duo by covering their song at the ACM Awards.

"My Songs Know What You Did in the Dark" by Fall Out Boy

At the Victoria's Secret Fashion Show, Taylor walked the runway to this song—revealing her pop-punk side that we would like to see more of!

"Jenny From The Block" by Jennifer Lopez

On her Red tour, Taylor brought J.Lo on stage for a fun rendition of this hit.

"Someone Like You" by Adele

Taylor sang a duet of this song with a leukemia patient that brought everyone to tears.

Taylor's Best Song Covers

Aside from being a storytelling and songwriting machine, Taylor also has a knack of turning another artist's song into her own. Let's take a look at some of her best covers:

"Riptide" by Vance Joy

Taylor's piano cover at BBC1's Live Lounge was so moving, she later brought Vance Joy on tour with her.

"Fire and Rain" by James Taylor

A special duet with James Taylor showed Taylor's deep connection to the song.

"Drops of Jupiter" by Train

This cover was loved so much, it was included on the live album of the Speak Now World Tour.

"White Blank Page" by Mumford & Sons

Taylor's heartfelt rendition showcased her guitar skills and emotional depth.

"Dancing in the Dark/Livin' on a Prayer" by Bruce Springsteen & Bon Jovi

An unexpected medley that left both Taylor and her fans thrilled.

"Untouchable" by Luna Halo

Taylor turned this rock song into a beautiful ballad, giving it a new life.

Build a Taylor Swift Concert

Right now, you're not just a fan—you will be the mastermind behind the most epic Taylor Swift concert ever imagined. Let's make a night so unforgettable, it can only exist in the wildest dreams of fans around the globe!

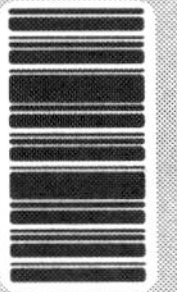

Pick the Venue

- Spectacular Stadium
- Intimate Theater
- Outdoor Festival
- Surprise Location (Your choice!):

Choose the Era: Which Taylor Swift era sets the theme for your show?

- Debut Delights
- Fearless Fantasy
- Speak Now Sparkle
- Red Romance
- 1989 Neon Nights
- Reputation's Edge
- Lover's Dream
- Folklore/Evermore Enchanted Forest
- Midnights Mystique

Dream Setlist: Pick 5 songs that are must-plays at your concert!

♫ ____________________

♫ ____________________

♫ ____________________

♫ ____________________

♫ ____________________

Feel free to mix and match across albums!

Surprise Guest Appearance: Who's joining Taylor on stage for a once-in-a-lifetime duet?

- Another Pop Icon: ________________
- A Legendary Rockstar: ________________
- An Up-and-Coming Artist: ________________
- A Fan from the Audience: ________________

The Encore: What's the one song Taylor closes the show with, leaving everyone breathless?

You've just built the ultimate Taylor Swift concert. Look back at your choices and imagine the magic, the music, and the memories being made. Keep this page as a reminder of the show that would shake the Swiftie universe to its core!

Now, Draw Your Outfit!

Tonight's the night and the only thing left to do is decide on your perfect concert outfit. Grab your pencils, markers, or whatever you love to create with, because it's time to bring your dream Taylor Swift concert outfit to life!

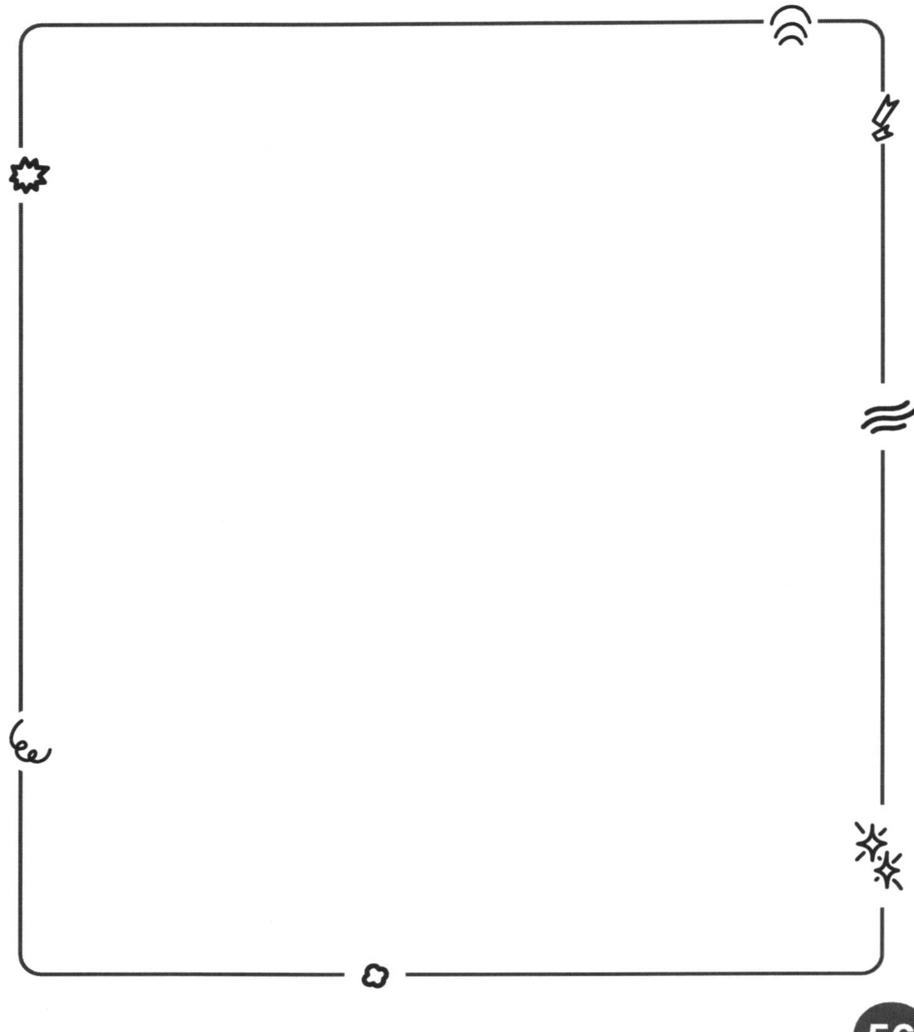

57

Taylor's Famous Collaborations

"ME!" with Brendon Urie (2019)

Taylor Swift's team-up with Brendon Urie of Panic! At The Disco on "ME!" introduced fans to a bubbly pop anthem that veered from Taylor's typical sound, introducing more fierce synth beats with a message of self-love.

"Safe & Sound" featuring The Civil Wars (2012)

For "The Hunger Games" soundtrack, Taylor joined forces with The Civil Wars to create "Safe & Sound," a haunting ballad that earned acclaim for its emotional depth—and perfectly embodying the vibe of Katniss Everdeen!

"Bad Blood" featuring Kendrick Lamar (2014)

Taylor's "Bad Blood" remix with Kendrick Lamar added an edgy, percussive layer to her album "1989," signaling a bold new era. Lamar's verses and the track's success at the Grammys and MTV VMAs proved the power of this pop-rap alliance.

"Highway Don't Care" with Tim McGraw and Keith Urban (2013)

Revisiting her country origins, Taylor collaborated with Tim McGraw and Keith Urban on "Highway Don't Care," a soulful narrative of love and longing.

Taylor's Famous Collaborations

"Exile" with Bon Iver (2020)

This song from "folklore" is a deep, emotive duet that explores the complexities of a failed relationship through beautifully interwoven vocals. Justin Vernon's raw, haunting voice alongside Taylor's clear, expressive tones—which instantly made it a fan-favorite.

"No Body, No Crime" featuring HAIM (2020)

Taylor's "evermore" album brought "No Body, No Crime" with HAIM, a country-rock tale of vengeanc that combined Swift's narrative songwriting with HAIM's distinctive sound.

"Everything Has Changed" with Ed Sheeran (2012)

Collaborating with Ed Sheeran, Swift explored new sonic territory on "Everything Has Changed," a gentle nod towards both artists' strengths in storytelling and acoustic sound, while hinting at Swift's evolving pop sensibilities.

"I Don't Wanna Live Forever" with Zayn (2017)

Taylor and Zayn Malik's "I Don't Wanna Live Forever" delivered an iconic duet that captivated listeners with its intense emotion and was celebrated as one of her standout soundtrack contributions.

Taylor's Musical Influences

Taylor Swift has always been open about the artists who have inspired her music, creating a fun mix of influences that you can hear in her songs. Let's take a closer look at the stars who have helped shape her sound.

Joni Mitchell

Joni Mitchell is a big one for Taylor, especially her album "**Blue**," which Taylor says explores "*somebody's soul so deeply*." The similarity in their songwriting is clear; both share a talent for diving into personal experiences with their lyrics.

Fall Out Boy

Fall Out Boy might not be the first band you'd associate with Taylor Swift, but she's called them one of her biggest lyrical inspirations. When announcing "**Speak Now (Taylor's Version)**," she mentioned how much the band influenced her writing.

Shania Twain

Shania Twain is another trailblazer Taylor admires for making the leap from country to pop—a path Taylor herself has followed. In a 2021 TikTok, Taylor gave a nod to Shania, using her music to highlight how country girls can indeed go pop!

Paul McCartney

Paul McCartney is a huge inspiration for Taylor, not just for his music but for how he handles fame with grace. She's praised McCartney for his kindness and respectfulness, qualities she strives to embody in her own career.

QUIZ TIME!

Taylor Swift's Famous Collaborations & Influences!

Now that we all have that settled—let's put your knowledge to test by taking this quiz! Are you ready to prove yourself a Swiftie? Let's find out!

1. Who did Taylor Swift team up with for the pop anthem "ME!" in 2019?

   A. Ed Sheeran
   B. Brendon Urie
   C. Zayn Malik
   D. Kendrick Lamar

2. For which movie soundtrack did Taylor Swift and The Civil Wars collaborate on the song "Safe & Sound"?

   A. Twilight
   B. The Hunger Games
   C. Divergent
   D. The Fault in Our Stars

3. "Bad Blood" saw Taylor Swift collaborating with which artist to add a pop-rap twist to her album "1989"?

   A. Drake
   B. Kendrick Lamar
   C. Jay Z
   D. Eminem

4. In 2013, Taylor Swift revisited her country roots with "Highway Don't Care" alongside which artists?

   A. Tim McGraw and Keith Urban
   B. Faith Hill and Brad Paisley
   C. Carrie Underwood and Luke Bryan
   D. Miranda Lambert and Blake Shelton

5. Which 2020 song from the album "folklore" featured Taylor Swift in a duet with Bon Iver?

   A. "cardigan"
   B. "the 1"
   C. "exile"
   D. "betty"

QUIZ TIME!

Taylor Swift's Famous Collaborations & Influences!

6 "No Body, No Crime" featuring HAIM is a part of which Taylor Swift album?

- A Lover
- B Reputation
- C Evermore
- D Folklore

7 Who did Taylor Swift collaborate with on "Everything Has Changed," marking a move towards evolving pop sensibilities?

- A Harry Styles
- B Ed Sheeran
- C Shawn Mendes
- D Justin Bieber

8 "I Don't Wanna Live Forever" was a powerful duet between Taylor Swift and which artist?

- A Sam Smith
- B Zayn Malik
- C Justin Timberlake
- D The Weeknd

9 Which artist is known to be a big influence on Taylor Swift, especially noted for the album "Blue"?

- A Carol King
- B Joni Mitchell
- C Stevie Nicks
- D Dolly Parton

10 Taylor Swift has mentioned which band as one of her biggest lyrical inspirations?

- A Green Day
- B The Beatles
- C Fall Out Boy
- D Maroon 5

How Well Do Your Friends Know Taylor?

Challenge your friends with our special Taylor Swift quiz, made just for her biggest fans!

Plus, you'll get a free 55-page Taylor Swift activity book that you'll only find in this book!

Scan the QR code or use the link below to see who's the ultimate fan now!

www.swiftiesuperfans.com/freebies

Taylor's Love For Secret Messages

Taylor Swift's career is a treasure trove of secret messages, hidden meanings, and cryptic clues, all of which her fans delight in deciphering. Here are five instances that showcase Swift's ingenious use of secret messages:

Capital Letters in CD Liners

Taylor started her tradition of hiding messages in her album liner notes with her early work. By capitalizing certain letters in the lyrics printed in her CD booklets, she spelled out secret messages to her fans. For instance, in "Fearless," the capital letters in "Fifteen" spell out "I CRIED WHILE RECORDING THIS."

Easter Eggs in Music Videos

Taylor's music videos are rich with hidden meanings and references. For example, in the video for "Look What You Made Me Do," Taylor includes numerous easter eggs, such as a throne of snakes and a dollar bill in a bathtub, each symbolizing different aspects of her public controversies and personal victories. In the "ME!" music video, you can also see the album name "Lover" in a pink neon sign!

Surprise Album Drops

Taylor surprised fans with the sudden release of "folklore" and "evermore" in 2020, a departure from her usual album release strategies. Before "folklore," she hinted at the album with an Instagram post captioned "Not a lot going on at the moment," a phrase she's used when there's actually something significant afoot.

Release Date Reveal in "Fearless" (Taylor's Version)

When announcing the re-release of "Fearless," Taylor teased fans with a cryptic message that had a random bunch of capital letters—which spelled out "APRIL NINTH," cleverly announcing the release date of the rerecorded album!

SPOT THE EASTER EGGS!

Turn the page around and have some fun spotting the easter eggs in this page!

The storefront's filled with a lot of things related to Taylor Swift—can you spot each and every single one of them? Spot the following things by drawing a circle around them—bonus points if you spot other easter eggs that aren't listed here, too!

The Art of Taylor's Lyrics

Taylor Swift has a special way of bringing her songs to life, and it all starts with how she imagines writing them. She shared her unique method during her speech at the Nashville Songwriter Awards, where she won Songwriter-Artist of the Decade. Taylor sorts her songs into three categories: Quill Pen, Fountain Pen, and Glitter Gel Pen lyrics, each representing a different vibe of her music.

Fountain Pen

Fountain Pen songs are modern tales of personal experiences, crafted like poetry. They're the kind of songs that stick with you, making you feel every emotion in vivid detail. Some examples include "**False God**" and "**Cruel Summer**" from her album "**Lover**", and "**exile**" featuring Bon Iver from "folklore". These songs are deep and thoughtful, often about moments and memories that are hard to forget.

Quill Pen

Then, there are the Quill Pen songs, which make you feel like you're stepping back in time. Taylor describes these as old-fashioned, likening them to what a 19th-century poet might write by candlelight. Tracks like "**ivy**" from "**evermore**" and "**my tears ricochet**" from "**folklore**" fit this category perfectly. They're rich with history and emotion, and they tell stories that feel timeless.

Glitter Gel Pen

Lastly, the Glitter Gel Pen songs are all about having fun. They're upbeat and make you want to dance and sing along. These tracks, like "**We Are Never Ever Getting Back Together**" from "**Red — Taylor's Version**" and "**You Need to Calm Down**" from "**Lover**", are reminders not to take life too seriously.

Fountain Pen Playlist

PLAY

SONG TITLE	ALBUM
The Archer	Lover
Cornelia Street	Lover
White Horse	Fearless – Taylor's Version
False God	Lover
Cruel Summer	Lover
Treacherous	Red – Taylor's Version
long story short	evermore
All Too Well (10 Minute version)	Red – Taylor's Version
State of Grace	Red – Taylor's Version
I Almost Do	Red – Taylor's Version
Holy Ground	Red – Taylor's Version
exile feat. Bon Iver	folklore
the 1	folklore
betty	folklore
champagne problems	evermore
marjorie	evermore
Lover	Lover
right where you left me	evermore

Quill Pen Playlist

PLAY

SONG TITLE	ALBUM
ivy	evermore
tolerate it	evermore
happiness	evermore
Carolina	Where the Crawdad's Sing soundtrack
evermore feat. Bon Iver	evermore
willow	evermore
cowboy like me	evermore
Sad Beautiful Tragic	Red – Taylor's Version
hoax	folklore
my tears ricochet	folklore
epiphany	folklore
the last great american dynasty	folklore
peace	folklore

Glitter Gel Pen Playlist

PLAY

SONG TITLE	ALBUM
I Forgot That You Existed	Lover
We Are Never Ever Getting Back Together	Red – Taylor's Version
Jump Then Fall	Fearless – Taylor's Version
22	Red – Taylor's Version
Today Was a Fairytale	Fearless – Taylor's Version
You Belong With Me	Fearless – Taylor's Version
I Think He Knows	Lover
London Boy	Lover
You Need to Calm Down	Lover
Hey Stephen	Fearless – Taylor's Version

The 6 Characters in 'folklore'

Taylor stunned the world thrice in 2020—when she released her surprise album 'folklore', then the sister album 'evermore', and showcasing a new kind of writing style: making songs about fictional characters or people in her life who have already passed away. Let's meet the characters alive in the 'folklore' universe:

James

A teenager caught in the throes of infidelity, James' summer affair sets the stage for a tale of remorse and redemption. Named after the daughter of Ryan Reynolds and Blake Lively, he seeks forgiveness from his girlfriend, Betty, in the heartfelt apology of "betty". Swift's creation of James' perspective offers a refreshing take on the theme of seeking forgiveness, highlighting the youthful folly of love and the desire for second chances.

Betty

The other half of the heartbroken duo, Betty narrates her side of the story in "cardigan", reflecting on the affair with a mix of wisdom and vulnerability. Also named after one of Reynolds and Lively's daughters, Betty's narrative weaves a complex portrait of young love, imbued with the foresight of experience and the hopeful naivety of youth. Through her eyes, listeners are reminded of the enduring power of love, despite the scars of betrayal.

Augustine

As "the other woman", Augustine's lament on "august" captures the ephemeral nature of her summer love with James. Her story, marked by longing and loss, contrasts with the deeper connection shared between James and Betty. Augustine's reflection on what could have been highlights the bittersweet reality of fleeting romances and the harsh truth of being the one left behind.

Inez

The bearer of truths, Inez serves as folklore's gossip, her words igniting the spark that reveals James' infidelity. Although she doesn't narrate her own song, Inez's role is important in the unraveling of the story, embodying the external forces that often influence the course of our relationships.

Rebekah Harkness

A bridge between Taylor's fictional realm and reality, Rebekah's legacy in "the last great american dynasty" mirrors Swift's own experiences with fame and judgment. Through Rebekah's story, Taylor explores themes of outsiderdom, rebellion, and the pursuit of authenticity in the face of societal expectations, drawing parallels between two women who refused to be defined by the narratives imposed upon them. And oh, she bought the house Rebekah lived in!

Dean

In "epiphany", Swift honors her grandfather Dean, a World War II veteran, drawing a poignant comparison between his silent sacrifices and the collective struggle against COVID-19. This track serves as a meditative reflection on the unspeakable horrors of war and the personal battles we face, reminding us of the strength found in quiet endurance and the power of unsung heroism.

Which Taylor Swift Song Character Are You?

Take this quiz to find out which character from Taylor Swift's "folklore" universe best represents you. Answer each question by choosing the option that resonates most with you. Tally your points according to the choices you make to discover which character you are!

What's your approach to love?

A	Full of regrets and seeking forgiveness	2 POINTS
B	Reflective, learning from past experiences	4 POINTS
C	Often find yourself dreaming of what could have been	3 POINTS
D	You tend to observe and comment rather than participate	1 POINT

How do you handle conflicts?

A	Apologize and try to make amends	2 POINTS
B	Reflect on both sides of the story	4 POINTS
C	Feel deeply, sometimes remaining in the background	3 POINTS
D	You're the one who often shares the truth with others	1 POINT

What role do you usually take in your group of friends?

A	The peacemaker, always trying to fix things	2 POINTS
B	The wise one, offering advice	4 POINTS
C	The dreamer, lost in your thoughts	3 POINTS
D	The storyteller, keeping everyone entertained with news	1 POINT

Choose a theme that resonates with you:

A	Redemption and forgiveness	2 POINTS
B	Love and resilience	4 POINTS
C	Longing and loss	3 POINTS
D	Truth and revelation	1 POINT

On a Friday night, you're most likely to be found:

A	Writing heartfelt apologies in your journal	2 POINTS
B	Wrapped in a cozy blanket, reflecting on past loves	4 POINTS
C	Looking at the stars, wondering about past summer flings	3 POINTS
D	Chatting away at a social gathering, sharing the latest gossip	1 POINT

Your dream vacation involves:

A	A quiet retreat where you can ponder on past actions	2 POINTS
B	A historical journey to places with rich stories and wisdom	4 POINTS
C	An escape to a romantic, secluded beach	3 POINTS
D	A visit to bustling cities known for their secrets and stories	1 POINT

In a movie about your life, what theme song plays in the background?

A	A melody of regret and hope for redemption	2 POINTS
B	A soulful tune reflecting growth and strength	4 POINTS
C	A haunting ballad of lost love and what-ifs	3 POINTS
D	A sharp, witty track that reveals hidden truths	1 POINT

What trait do you value most in others?

A	The courage to admit when they're wrong and strive to make things right	2 POINTS
B	The ability to see the best in people, even after being hurt	4 POINTS
C	A romantic heart, always hopeful despite past heartaches	3 POINTS
D	Honesty, even when it's hard to hear the truth	1 POINT

Results

8–11 Points | **Inez**

Like Inez, you have a knack for seeing and revealing the truth, making you a pivotal figure in your circle.

12–18 Points | **James**

Much like James, you've experienced growth through remorse and redemption, showing that everyone deserves a second chance.

19–25 Points | **Augustine**

Your essence aligns with Augustine, where you've known longing and loss, yet you carry a hopeful heart.

26–32 Points | **Betty**

Resilient and wise, you share Betty's strength in facing life's challenges, valuing love and forgiveness above all.

Taylor Swift Lyrics That Speak To Me

Taylor Swift has built an incredible collection of songs that connect deeply with people all over the globe. She excels in crafting lyrics that tell stories and express feelings, touching on everything from the joys of youth to thoughtful self-reflection. On this page, allow yourself to share how Taylor's songs resonate with your own experiences.

The Lyric That Feels Like Home
Write down a Taylor Swift lyric that feels like it was penned just for you. Share a memory or feeling this lyric evokes in you!

Soundtrack of My Life
If you could choose one Taylor Swift song to represent your life, which would it be? Describe a moment in your life that this song perfectly encapsulates.

Words of Wisdom
Jot down a lyric by Taylor Swift that has offered you comfort, guidance, or inspiration. How has this message influenced your perspective or decisions?

The Anthem of My Joy
Identify a Taylor Swift song that uplifts you or brings you joy.
Explain why this song is your go-to for feeling good!

A Melody for the Melancholy
Select a lyric that you turn to in times of sadness or reflection. How does this song or lyric provide comfort during tough times?

Future Echoes
Envision a future moment or achievement. Which Taylor Swift song do you imagine playing in the background? Explain why this song accompanies your vision of the future!

About Taylor Swift

Taylor 's mother, Andrea, chose the name "**Taylor**" for her daughter with a forward-thinking reason in mind. She wanted a name that wouldn't immediately reveal her gender to anyone who read it, highlighting a desire for gender neutrality and equal opportunities from the very start.

Taylor can play the guitar, piano, ukulele, electric guitar, and banjo, showcasing her broad musical talents and dedication to her craft.

Not only does Taylor have a talented younger brother, Austin Swift, but he also pursued higher education at Vanderbilt University. In addition to his academic pursuits, Austin is a freelance photographer, capturing the world through his lens in his free time.

Taylor took her talents to the big screen with a role in the 2010 film "**Valentine's Day**," where she played the character Felicia, adding film actress to her repertoire.

Taylor's grandmother was not just any singer; she was a professional opera singer. This remarkable family tie influenced Taylor from a young age, even inspiring her to incorporate her grandmother's singing into her song "**marjorie**."

Taylor lent her voice to the animated character Audrey in the film "**The Lorax**," bringing the character to life with her distinctive voice and adding voice actress to her list of achievements.

At just 11 years old, Taylor showcased her vocal talents at a Philadelphia 76ers basketball game, performing "**The Star-Spangled Banner**." Her early brush with the spotlight didn't stop there; she also clinched a win in a local talent competition with her rendition of LeAnn Rimes' "**Big Deal**."

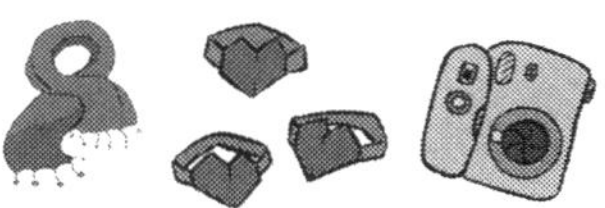

In a 2016 '**73 Questions**' video with Vogue, Taylor revealed a unique physical trait: she has double-jointed elbows.

Before the release of her groundbreaking album "**1989**," Taylor went above and beyond for her fans by inviting 89 of her biggest supporters to her house for an exclusive listening party. She also baked cookies for her guests, creating a once-in-a-lifetime experience for those lucky enough to attend.

Taylor's purchase of a holiday home in Rhode Island for $17.75 million led to an unexpected nickname for a state tax. Dubbed the "**Taylor Swift Tax**," this levy applies to those with second homes in the state valued over $2 million.

A well-known cat lover, Taylor Swift's three feline friends each bear names inspired by characters from popular culture. Olivia Benson is named after a character from "**Law and Order: Special Victims Unit**," Meredith Grey from "**Grey's Anatomy**," and Benjamin Button, who she adopted after being featured in the music video for "**Me!**", is of course named after "**The Curious Case of Benjamin Button**."

Taylor's songwriting process is as mystical as it is talented; she has shared that some of her songs' lyrics and melodies come to her in dreams. After dreaming these creative snippets, she wakes up and hastily records them, either writing them down on whatever she can find or recording voice memos on her phone.

Taylor has a unique way of organizing the emotional journey of her albums, notably by placing one of her most emotional songs in the fifth spot on the tracklist. This strategic placement has made the fifth track a significant marker for fans.

Despite her fearless persona in music and life, Taylor has admitted to having a peculiar fear: **sea urchins!**

Taylor's Most Inspirational Quotes

"No matter what happens in life, be good to people. Being good to people is a wonderful legacy to leave behind."

"Just be yourself, there is no one better."

"The lesson I've learned the most often in life is that you're always going to know more in the future than you know now."

"When I was a little girl I used to read fairy tales. In fairy tales you meet Prince Charming and he's everything you ever wanted. In fairy tales the bad guy is very easy to spot. The bad guy is always wearing a black cape so you always know who he is. Then you grow up and you realize that Prince Charming is not as easy to find as you thought. You realize the bad guy is not wearing a black cape and he's not easy to spot; he's really funny, and he makes you laugh, and he has perfect hair."

"To me, Fearless is not the absence of fear. It's not being completely unafraid. To me, Fearless is having fears. Fearless is having doubts. Lots of them. To me, Fearless is living in spite of those things that scare you to death."

"Everybody has that point in their life where you hit a crossroads and you've had a bunch of bad days and there's different ways you can deal with it and the way I dealt with it was I just turned completely to music."

"There's more to life than dating the boy on the football team."

"If you're horrible to me, I'm going to write a song about it, and you won't like it. That's how I operate."

"You can walk away and say 'We don't need this,' but something in your eyes says 'We can beat this.'"

"I've wanted one thing for me whole life and I'm not going to be that girl who wants one thing her whole life then gets it and complains."

"I've learned that you can't predict [love] or plan for it. For someone like me who is obsessed with organization and planning, I love the idea that love is the one exception to that. Love is the one wild card."

"I've found time can heal most anything and you just might find who you're supposed to be."

"At some point you have to forget about grudges because they only hurt."

"Be that strong girl that everyone knew would make it through the worst, be that fearless girl, the one who would dare to do anything, be that independent girl who didn't need a man; be that girl who never backed down."

"Never believe anyone who tells you that you don't deserve what you want."

Can't get enough of what you've learned about Taylor?

Turn this page for more bonus content!

Let's Play Some Crossword

Across

4. The first album she released during the pandemic.
6. In Taylor's Versions, she calls the extra song as ones From The _____.
10. A song where you can hear Taylor's heartbeat in the background.
11. The 5th song of 'Reputation.'
13. She is Taylor's first cat; named after a character in 'Grey's Anatomy'

Down

1. Taylor's favorite number.
2. Taylor's middle name.
3. Fans loved this song so much Taylor released a ten-minute version of it!
5. This is the first album rerecording that she released in 2021.
7. A singer featured in 'Snow on the Beach.'
8. Her 10th studio album released in 2022.
9. The last track in Speak Now (Taylor's Version).
12. What Taylor calls her fans.

Across

2. A month; Taylor did a cover of this famous song on Spotify.
7. This was supposed to be the tour name of 'Lover.'
11. A darker shade of red; a song from 'Midnights.'
12. Taylor has written and released three songs with him.
13. 'We found ___________, you and I got lost in it.'

Down

1. A street mentioned in one of the songs from 'Lover.'
3. A song from 'Speak Now' which was also supposed to be the original title of the said album.
4. He sang 'I Don't Wanna Live Forever' together with Taylor.
5. It is believed that the song 'Style' is about this pop singer; ex-boyband member.
6. Taylor grew up on a ___________ Tree Farm.
8. The only song title in 'Fearless' with a name on it.
9. A song title from 'folklore' that is also a piece of clothing.
10. A song of Taylor's for 'Where the Crawdads Sing.'

Bake Like Taylor!

Aside from being a killer singer and songwriter, Taylor is also quite known for whipping up baked goods to give to her family, friends, and fans! Here are some recipes of hers that you can make on your own while listening to her albums:

Taylor Recipe #1 Chai Sugar Cookies With Eggnog Icing

What You Need

Before we begin, ensure your kitchen is stocked with:

- **Butter and Oil**
  A duo of softened unsalted butter and neutral oil for tender cookies.
- **Sugars**
  Granulated for sweetness, powdered for moisture control and chewiness.
- **Basics**
  All-purpose flour, baking soda, and kosher salt.
- **The Spice of Life**
  Chai's signature comes from ground ginger, cinnamon, allspice, cardamom, cloves, and black pepper.
- **Bind and Flavor**
  An egg and a splash of vanilla extract.
- **Glaze Goodness**
  Powdered sugar and nutmeg, mixed with milk or eggnog for the perfect finish.

Let's Bake!!

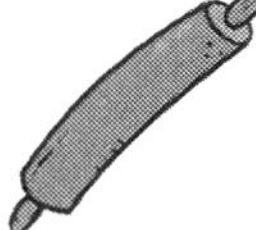

1. **Smooth Start**
Begin by whipping the butter to ensure it's soft and welcoming.

2. **Blend in Oils**
Mix in the oil with the butter. It's okay if they don't fully combine.

3. **Sugar and Spice**
Add the sugars and spices, blending them with the butter and oil for a mix full of flavor.

4. **Wet into Dry**
Stir in the egg and vanilla, then gradually mix in the dry ingredients to form a soft, malleable dough.

5. **Chill Out**
Give the dough a rest in the fridge for an hour to firm up and develop the flavors.

Shaping, Baking, and Glazing

1. **Shape It Up**
With chilled dough, form two tablespoon-sized portions into thick disks.

2. **Sugar Coat**
Roll each disk in cinnamon sugar for an extra flavor layer.

3. **Oven Time**
Space the cookies on a lined baking sheet and bake until they're just right.

4. **Glaze on Top**
Mix the glaze ingredients and drizzle over cooled cookies for that final touch!

Taylor Recipe #2 Spaghetti and Meatballs Special

What You Need

- **Meats for the Meatballs**
  1 pound of ground beef, 1/2 pound each of ground pork and ground veal blend for tender, flavorful meatballs.

- **Breadcrumbs for Binding**
  1 cup of fresh white breadcrumbs (feel free to use sandwich bread or buns) and 1/4 cup of seasoned bread crumbs for added flavor.

- **Seasonings and Cheese**
  Fresh chopped parsley (2 tablespoons), freshly grated Parmesan cheese (1/2 cup), kosher salt, black pepper, and a hint of ground nutmeg for depth.

- **The Binder**
  1 large egg, beaten, to hold everything together.
  Moisture for Mixing: 3/4 cup of warm water to combine the ingredients smoothly without overworking the meat.

Preparing...

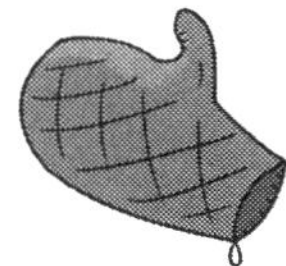

1. **Mixing the Meatballs**
   In a large bowl, combine the meats, both breadcrumbs, parsley, Parmesan, salt, pepper, nutmeg, and the egg. Gently stir in the warm water. Mixing with your hands is the best way to ensure just the right consistency without overworking the mixture.

2. **Forming the Meatballs**
   Shape the mixture into 2-inch meatballs and place them on a plate. Expect to make about 16 to 18 meatballs.

3. **Browning the Meatballs**
   Heat a mix of vegetable and olive oil in a large skillet over medium heat. Cook the meatballs in batches until they're nicely browned on all sides. Transfer them to a paper towel-lined baking sheet to drain.

Cooking the Sauce and Meatballs

1. **Sautéing Onions and Garlic**
   In the same skillet, add a bit more olive oil and cook chopped onions until translucent. Add minced garlic and cook until fragrant. Then, pour in the red wine, letting it simmer until reduced.

2. **Creating the Tomato Sauce**
   Add crushed tomatoes to the skillet, seasoning with parsley, salt, and pepper. Stir well and let it simmer for a few minutes.

3. **Simmering the Meatballs**
   Return the meatballs to the skillet, cover, and cook on low heat for 25-30 minutes, stirring occasionally to ensure even cooking.

Plate a generous serving of spaghetti, top with meatballs and sauce, and finish with a sprinkle of freshly grated Parmesan cheese. It's a dish meant to be savored slowly, where every bite brings you closer to the heartwarming essence of Taylor Swift's home cooking!

Let's Do Some Word Search!

T	M	M	H	S	F	Q	T	N	D	K	W	R	F	T
F	A	U	C	Z	V	O	P	Z	I	A	G	R	S	I
Y	F	O	X	Y	J	H	F	Q	Y	F	I	W	I	X
L	L	A	V	E	N	D	E	R	H	A	Z	E	O	B
A	U	E	N	C	I	T	K	M	F	U	Z	R	K	T
L	A	I	W	R	V	X	Z	J	A	R	K	O	C	M
Z	S	N	L	U	U	W	E	P	W	E	D	L	W	U
G	O	R	G	E	O	U	S	L	F	P	S	K	C	V
T	C	Q	M	L	Z	H	D	P	D	U	N	L	S	Q
A	Y	E	L	S	E	D	G	W	E	T	E	O	K	C
V	W	I	Z	U	S	S	E	L	R	A	E	F	R	G
X	W	F	I	M	R	W	O	U	N	T	K	E	A	L
U	P	C	H	M	M	V	D	G	F	I	V	N	K	Y
K	P	C	C	E	E	V	E	R	M	O	R	E	O	M
C	G	Y	X	R	S	T	H	G	I	N	D	I	M	W

CLEAN
CRUELSUMMER
EVERMORE
FEARLESS
FOLKLORE
GORGEOUS
LAVENDERHAZE

LOVER
MIDNIGHTS
RED
REPUTATION
SPEAKNOW
WILLOW

Let's Do Some Word Search!

Y	M	F	A	W	S	X	M	J	B	L	T	S	R	N
B	I	A	F	Y	L	P	A	T	L	A	M	R	A	K
F	R	N	T	O	O	O	A	N	A	U	Q	I	O	E
D	R	B	E	T	T	Y	V	R	N	G	U	K	J	J
D	O	B	R	N	K	I	Y	E	K	U	P	I	G	E
A	R	G	G	D	D	R	E	S	S	S	H	T	S	I
Y	B	O	L	T	N	G	D	K	P	T	F	R	X	S
L	A	L	O	A	K	F	A	F	A	D	O	L	Y	Z
I	L	D	W	D	C	J	S	M	C	H	F	R	Y	X
G	L	R	N	C	I	C	W	R	E	T	S	O	Y	Y
H	C	U	O	T	C	I	R	T	C	E	L	E	B	M
T	I	S	M	R	V	F	I	F	Z	Z	K	H	P	U
U	Q	H	O	L	F	H	C	O	Q	I	Y	Z	U	Q
R	K	J	E	D	W	N	C	V	W	Y	A	Z	J	V
I	Z	V	A	H	R	U	C	T	K	S	P	S	S	D

AFTERGLOW
AUGUST
BETTY
BLANKSPACE
DAYLIGHT
DRESS
ELECTRICTOUCH
ENDGAME

GOLDRUSH
KARMA
LOVESTORY
MIRRORBALL
SHAKEITOFF
SPARKSFLY
WHITEHORSE

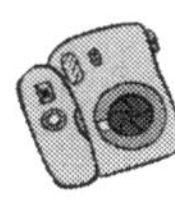

How To Create The Ultimate Swiftie Playlist

Ready to make your own musical diary courtesy of Taylor's lyrical masterpieces? Let's create a playlist of 13 songs, capturing the highs and lows, the sparkles and shadows of life—with each song a piece of the puzzle that is you!

1 **Pick Your Mood Starter:** Are you feeling dreamy, reflective, or ready to dance? Kick off your playlist with a song that matches your current mood.

2 **Flashback Favorite:** Choose a Taylor song that takes you back to a happy moment. What memory does it spark?

3 **Heartbreak Healer:** We've all had our hearts bruised. Which Taylor song helps you heal or feel understood?

4 **Dance It Out:** Which of Taylor's songs makes you want to dance around your room? Add it to your list!

5 **Lyric Love:** Find a Taylor lyric that you adore or live by. Which song is it from? Add that song next.

6 **Friendship Anthem:** Taylor sings about friendships too. Pick a song that reminds you of your bestie.

7 **The Underdog:** Is there a Taylor song you think deserves more love? Give it a spot on your playlist.

8 **Dreamy Duet:** Taylor's duets are magical. Choose your favorite for a touch of collaboration magic.

9 **Soulful Slowdown:** Select a slower, soulful song for those moments when you need to unwind or reflect.

10 **Empowerment Encore:** End your playlist with a powerful Taylor anthem that leaves you feeling strong and unstoppable.

11 **Secret Storyteller:** Taylor's knack for storytelling is unmatched. Choose a song that tells a story you can't get out of your head.

12 **Nostalgic Notes:** Pick a song that fills you with nostalgia, one that takes you to a place or feeling you cherish.

13 **Midnight Melody:** Which Taylor song is perfect for those late-night moments, when the world is quiet and you're lost in thought?

What I Would Say To Taylor Swift

Dear Swiftie, you've journeyed through facts, quotes, trivia, and the magical universe of Taylor Swift. Now, it's your turn to share a piece of your heart. Imagine standing face to face with Taylor Swift, the artist who has inspired, uplifted, and accompanied you through different seasons of your life. What would you say to her? How has her music touched your life? What song lyrics have become your mantras? Here's your space to express your thoughts, gratitude, stories, and maybe even dreams you hope to achieve, inspired by Taylor's journey. Let your heart speak!

Love,

Answer Key

Quiz Time! How Well Do You Know Young Taylor?

1. B
2. B
3. C
4. C
5. B

Quiz Time! Guess The Taylor Swift Album

1. Red
2. Fearless
3. 1989
4. folklore
5. Reputation
6. Lover
7. Speak Now
8. Taylor Swift
9. Midnights
10. folklore

Quiz Time! Taylor's Tour Trivia

1. B
2. B
3. B
4. A
5. B
6. C
7. B
8. B
9. C
10. C

Quiz Time: Taylor Swift's Famous Collaborations & Influences!

1. B
2. B
3. B
4. A
5. C
6. C
7. B
8. B
9. B
10. C

Crossword 1:

Across
4. FOLKLORE
6. VAULT
10. WILDESTDREAMS
11. DELICATE
13. MEREDITH

Down
1. THIRTEEN
2. ALISON
3. ALLTOOWELL
5. FEARLESS
7. LANADELREY
8. MIDNIGHTS
9. TIMELESS
12. SWIFTIES

Crossword 2:

Across
2. SEPTEMBER
7. LOVERFEST
11. MAROON
12. EDSHEERAN
13. WONDERLAND

Down
1. CORNELIA
3. ENCHANTED
4. ZAYNMALIK
5. HARRYSTYLES
6. CHRISTMAS
8. HEYSTEPHEN
9. CARDIGAN
10. CAROLINA

Claim Your Free 55-Page Taylor Swift Activity Book!

We adore Taylor and her fans just as much as you do!

That's why we're offering a unique 55-page bonus activity book exclusively just for you.

You won't find this book anywhere else! Don't miss out.

Scan the QR code or click the link below to download your special gift now!

www.swiftiesuperfans.com/freebies

Made in the USA
Columbia, SC
30 November 2024